Not everyone is a morning person. I get that. But I have learned that when I start my day off with God everything is just plain better.

I realize that some people work nights, or different shifts. So, if that's you, this devotional time might take place in the afternoon. Whenever you wake up, this devotional will be the first thing you do. Plan on doing this for 31 days. It is said that it takes 21 days to create a habit. Some say it takes longer. Whatever your schedule, today seems like a good time to get going on a life altering habit.

When you wake up DO NOT pick up your phone. If your phone serves as your alarm simply shut the alarm off and put the phone down. No distractions. These scriptures are all taken from my book Hope Against Hope, Living your life so that no trial is wasted. They are all in that book because they have had a profound impact on my life. They have been life giving to me, and I pray they will be life giving to you as well.

Grab your Bible and a cup of coffee, find a cozy spot, and talk to God for a few. Plan on spending a minimum of 15 minutes with Him. I realize that for some 15 minutes is a very long time, while for others it's way too short. You can adjust the time spent as you need to. But please don't go below 15 minutes. You can do this! Be sure to make this the first thing you do every single day! Congrats on diving into a deeper relationship with Him.

Libbie

DAY ONE

Read -

Isaiah 61:1-1-3

The spirit of the sovereign Lord is on me, because the Lord has anointed me to preach good news to the poor. He has sent me to bind up the brokenhearted, to proclaim freedom for the captives and release from darkness for the prisoners, to proclaim the year of the Lord's favor and the day of vengeance of our God, to comfort all who mourn, and provide for those who grieve in Zion - to bestow on them a crown of beauty instead of ashes, the oil of joy instead of mourning, and a garment of praise instead of a spirit of despair. They will be called oaks of righteousness, a planting of the Lord for the display of his splendor.

Thoughts -

It's easy to feel like someone else will do it. Someone else will help them, feed them, love them, tell them about Jesus. But He has given every one of us the directive to go and be the church to the world around us. In January 2019 God put Isaiah 61 on my heart as my own life mission statement. I have embraced it, I know that He has called me to preach the good news, set the captives free, heal the broken hearted, and tell people that they are children of God...oaks of righteousness. That seems like a really tall order. So I'm taking it one step at a time. I started by writing Hope Against Hope. Now I'm writing this devotional. Not sure what will be next, but I'm watching and listening for His direction. What would He have you do with what He has given you? It doesn't have to be grandiose. It doesn't have to be a major change in your life. What is he speaking to your heart about reaching those around you?

Pray -

Lord, Your Spirit is alive in me. You have set me apart, created me for a purpose. I want to get closer to You so I can begin to understand what that purpose is. As I draw close to You, will you come close to me? For the next month I'm going to show up here, Lord. Will you meet me here? And will you lead me today, Lord? I will follow. In Jesus name, amen.

Be Still -

Now just sit quietly with God, think about the scripture you read, re-read it if need be. Spend the rest of the 15 minutes just being with God.

DAY TWO

Read -
Proverbs 31:4-9

It is not for kings, Lemuel - it is not for kings to drink wine, not for rulers to crave beer, lest they drink and forget what has been decreed, and deprive all the oppressed of their rights. Let beer be for those who are perishing, wine for those who are in anguish! Let them drink and forget their poverty and remember their misery no more. Speak up for those who cannot speak for themselves, for the rights of all who are destitute. Speak up and judge fairly; defend the rights of the poor and needy.

Thoughts -

This scripture holds two very important truths for me. The first is that I cannot allow any substance to have a foothold in my life. Maybe alcohol is not an issue for you, maybe for you it's something else. Perhaps pornography? Maybe food? Maybe social media? You know what it is, now is your time to overcome. Nothing can own you unless you allow it to. So make a choice to no longer allow it to own you. I realize my words can be frustrating. If you cannot set that thing aside without help then get the help you need to do so. If it's really big, seek professional help. If it's a little smaller, tell someone you trust, ask them to hold you accountable. Just do it.

The second truth this scripture holds for me is that I am most definitely called to speak up for those who cannot speak up for themselves. Honestly, I'm not entirely sure what that looks like in my life. I spend time counseling with women who need hope. I know I've been called to do that. I share the gospel every chance I get. I'm currently asking God to show me where I fit in when it comes to defending the rights of the poor and needy. What has He put on your heart?

Pray -

Jesus, if I am totally honest, _____ has more control over my life than I would like to admit. I spend my time, energy and focus on it far more than I should. Today I lay it down at your feet, Jesus. Would you take it? Would you give me wisdom to know what steps I need to take to completely eradicate its control over my life? And Lord, as I get a handle on my life, would you begin to open my eyes to the needs of others around me? Show me where I can bring justice, hope, grace and truth. In Your name.

Be Still -

Now just sit quietly with God, think about the scripture you read, re-read it if need be. Spend the rest of the

15 minutes just being with God.

DAY THREE

Read -
Proverbs 3:5-6

Trust in the Lord with all your heart and lean not on your own understanding; in all your ways submit to him, and he will make your paths straight.

Thoughts -

This scripture has walked me through some very dark times. If you read Hope Against Hope you know there were days when all I could pray was, "I trust You." The awesome thing is...that prayer was enough. When I was working on this devotional I decided to read this scripture from my Amplified Bible.

Here's how it reads:
Lean on, trust in, and be **confident** in the Lord with all your heart and mind. Do not rely on your own insight or understanding. In all your ways know, recognize, and acknowledge Him, and He will direct and make straight and **plain** your paths.

Wow. I'm not sure why I am always amazed at what God

does. I mean, I know He's a big God. I know He cares about me and my little life. But I am always shocked when He reaches down to touch my life. That's exactly what He did with this scripture. As I said above, this scripture has walked me through some dark times. But here I am in the middle of some not-so-dark but rather uncertain times and I can't seem to steady myself. But here God reminded me that I can be confident because of Him. I can continue to walk with one foot in front of the other through my daily life and He will make plain my paths.

Is there an area of your life that you are uncertain in? Perhaps you just keep looking the other way because it's easier than facing it. Be confident in who God is and who He has made you to be. Allow Him to make plain your paths today.

Pray -

Lord, today I choose to trust You in every situation. I trust You with my whole life. I choose confidence today. Not in myself or my ability, but rather in your plans and who You have made me to be. Direct, make straight and plain my path today, Lord, and I will walk it. In Jesus name.

Be Still -

Now just sit quietly with God, think about the scripture you read, re-read it if need be. Spend the rest of the 15 minutes just being with God.

DAY FOUR

Read -
Ezekiel 36:26

I will give you a new heart and put a new spirit in you; I will remove from you your heart of stone and give you a heart of flesh.

Thoughts -

Boy have I seen God do this in my own life. As a young person, my heart desired everything of this world. My spirit was not aligned with God's in any way. It didn't alert me when I was exposing myself to ungodliness. My old heart and my old spirit allowed me to consume things which led me on a path to eternal destruction and damnation. Pretty strong statement, huh? It's true, though. It really is. When we hunger for and are satiated with the things of this world our spirit ends up dead and lost. But when we run to Jesus He puts a new heart and a new spirit in us. 2 Corinthians 5:17 says that we are new creations in Christ and the old us is gone. The new heart He gives us begins to desire Him and the things that point us to Him. The new spirit begins to alert us when we are filling up on things that are not good for us. Why? Because when we choose to follow Christ, the one who loves us beyond what we can fathom, the Holy Spirit resides inside of us...and that changes everything.

Perhaps you are watching someone you love run after the desires of their heart that are the opposite of what God would want. Maybe your heart breaks as you pray for their spirit to warn them of the dangers ahead. I struggled with seeing my son choose everything but God. In my brokenness I cried out to God to rescue him. I asked for a new heart and a new spirit for this boy that I love so deeply, knowing full well that God loves him even more. Who do you need to pray for today? Your child? Your parents? A friend? Or is it you? There's a brand new heart and brand new spirit waiting to be had.

Pray -

Lord Jesus, I can see the need for a softened heart, a heart that desires what You love. I can see a need for a spirit that is led by Yours, a spirit that stops us from stepping into sin and destruction. I know that _____ needs these things right now. Would you put a new heart in _____ today, Lord? One that feels what You feel, loves what You love and wants what You want. Would you give them/me a new spirit? One that is in tune with your plan and your will. One that is led by Your Holy Spirit into Your purpose. In Jesus name.

Be Still -

Now just sit quietly with God, think about the scripture you read, re-read it if need be. Spend the rest of the 15 minutes just being with God

DAY FIVE

Read -
Psalm 139:7-10

Where can I go from your Spirit? Where can I flee from your presence? If I go up to the heavens, you are there, if i make my bed in the depths, you are there, if I rise on the wings of the dawn, if I settle on the far side of the sea, even there your hand will guide me, your right hand will guide me, your right hand will hold me fast.

Thoughts -

Have you been running from God? Maybe completely, maybe you are just trying to pretend He is not there so you can go on about your life the way you want. Or maybe it's just one little area that you have hidden from Him. Maybe that thing is non negotiable to you. Like, you'll go to church and even serve, but this thing cannot be discussed.

But here's the truth, if you don't hand it over He can't have all of you, and if He can't have all of you, you can't be fully who He has called you to be. Yeah, read that again. That one thing is stopping you from becoming all God has called you to be. The next verse in this chapter goes on to talk about how God Himself created you with His very own hand. He most definitely has good plans for you, my friend.

Do you want all He has for you? It's time to stop running. Do you want to grow and excel? It's time to surrender it all...everything. Yes, even that thing. He sees it anyway. He knows it's there. Open your hand.

Pray -

Lord, I don't want to live with my fists clenched tightly holding to what I think is mine. I want everything You have for me. I want to be the person You created me to be. So, this morning, I hand over _____. It's Yours. Today, I stop running and hiding. I know that wherever I go you are there, there is no hiding from You. So I step out into full view today, God. I'm fully Yours. Make me what you created me to be. In Jesus' name, amen.

Be Still -

Now just sit quietly with God, think about the scripture you read, re-read it if need be. Spend the rest of the 15 minutes just being with God.

DAY SIX

Read -
Psalm 51:1-2

Have mercy on me, O God, according to your unfailing love; according to your great compassion blot out my transgressions. Wash away all my iniquity and cleanse me from my sin.

Thoughts -

We may read this scripture and think it is saying the same thing in three ways. But it is not. To sin is to miss the mark, to fall short of the glory of God. To transgress is to choose to intentionally disobey. It is willfully stepping over the line. We see a very clear example of this in the story of David and Bathsheba. David should not have been looking at Bathsheba while she was bathing. He willfully stepped over the line of guarding his heart and eyes and it led to the sin of an affair with Bathsheba, which led to iniquity. Iniquity is a premeditated choice. David planned out how to kill Bathsheba's husband. Yikes.

This scripture is literally covering everything. It was

actually written after the prophet Nathan came to David to call him out for his sin with Bathsheba and the iniquity of having her husband killed. David was broken down completely before God. He laid it all out and said, "God, I did this. I stepped over the line. I transgressed, then I sinned, then in my iniquity I literally had a man killed. But I know those things aren't too much for You, Lord. Forgive me, please, have mercy on me." He even goes on to say that he realizes his sins are really only against God, when all God wants from us is faithfulness. Ouch. When we look at our choices in light of that, in light of what God wants from us, in light of who our behavior honors or goes against, it should cause us to pause. I mean, He is merciful, He does forgive. But when does our own transgression, sin and iniquity build a wall so big that we are able to pretend He's not even there? He never walks away from us in our sin. But we run from Him. And we could run so fast and far that we don't look back.

I am grateful that somehow He has made me able to see over the walls I have built with my own sin. I have been able to hear God calling me back from my own messes. I pray that every time I add a brick to those walls I am aware enough to pull it back down. My prayer is the same for my children, because they will sin. They will cross lines and make poor choices. It is inevitable. We all do. So pray for those you love, ask God to send people like Nathan to call them out and call them up.

Pray -
Lord, forgive me of every transgression, every sin,

every iniquity. Keep me close to you, Lord. I do not want to live this life without Your presence. Moses knew the promised land was nothing if You didn't go with them. I know that my life is nothing if You aren't leading me. And for _____, Lord, would you send a Nathan to help them see where they are missing it? Would you have mercy on them, God. Bring them to repentance and forgiveness, In Jesus name.

Be Still -

Now just sit quietly with God, think about the scripture you read, re-read it if need be. Spend the rest of the 15 minutes just being with God

DAY SEVEN

Read -
Zephaniah 3:17

The Lord your God is with you, the Mighty Warrior who saves. He will take great delight in you; in his love he will no longer rebuke you, but will rejoice over you with singing.

Thoughts -

I love, love this scripture. I love that no matter what I am walking through He is there. The Lord, my God, is with me. And not only is He with me, He is THE Mighty Warrior who saves. Not just one of the mighty warriors. THE mightiest of them all. THE Mighty Warrior who saves. Whoah. Stop and really think about that for a minute.

AND He is with me. He is right here. As I walk through any struggle, He is right here. Even though I screw up repeatedly He takes great delight in me and no longer rebukes me. Rather, He rejoices over me with singing. I totally get that concept. I rejoice over my kids with singing all the time. I have since they were born. Their entire lives have been filled with songs I have made up, songs from the radio, worship songs. I sing to them, over them, with them. And the thought of God doing the same for me makes my heart swell. I know how much I love my kids, and He loves me far more. He is literally delighted with me. My mistakes do not put an end to His delight. Why? Because He sees the end from the beginning. He knew I would make those mistakes before He ever made me. He still called me. He still loves me. He knows I will overcome. It is only by Him that I can. And yes, it hurts His heart when I make bad choices. But He loves me all the same. He waits for me to reach for Him. He responds to me with love - - rejoices over me with singing.

There's a song by Hillsong United called Highlands. I absolutely love the lyrics to this song. They are incredible lyricists anyway, but this one reaches into the depths of the soul. I'm sharing only the chorus here, but the verses are just as amazing, so go listen to it. But check this chorus out:

So I will praise You on the mountain
And I will praise You when the mountain's in my way
You're the summit where my feet are
So I will praise You in the valleys all the same
No less God within the shadows
No less faithful when the night leads me astray
You're the heaven where my heart is
In the highlands and the heartache all the same

Yeah, He is no less God within the shadows of our lives. His faithfulness doesn't change just because we have gone astray. He is the same yesterday, today and forever. I am grateful.

Pray -

Lord, Your faithfulness overwhelms me. I am eternally grateful for who You are...for the love and grace You extend far beyond what I deserve. Today I want to just be with You. I want to sit here and remember just how good You are, Lord. When I have run You have chased me. When I have sinned You have forgiven. Thank you, Jesus, for who You are...the mightiest of all warriors. Thank You for saving me.

Be Still -

Now just sit quietly with God, think about the scripture you read, re-read it if need be. Spend the rest of the 15 minutes just being with God

DAY EIGHT

Read -
Luke 16:10

Whoever can be trusted with very little can also be trusted with much, and whoever is dishonest with very little will also be dishonest with much.

Thoughts -

In my book, Hope Against Hope, I shared this scripture with a story about a little youth camp I was taking our youth band to so they could lead worship. I shared that there were many frustrations over actually getting a band there to do it. I shared how a friend suggested I just cancel, and how I believed God was saying for me to be faithful with the little camp He had entrusted to me. I also said that I don't necessarily think I will be leading big things, but that it was just a principle He was pointing me to.

As I sit here and read this scripture again...as I look at the ministry opportunities God has given me as recent as today...I know He is actually preparing me for the big things. Not the big events with many people, but rather the one on one conversations with a broken heart

- those are big things to Him. In His upside down kingdom, the one person is the big thing. I have to laugh that I haven't seen this before. Of course one person is a big thing to Him. He is the one who leaves the 99 to go after the one. Why? Because one soul, one life, one person is a really big deal to Him. One person should be a really big deal to us too.

I sat at coffee this morning across the table from a woman who has been set free from a horrible past. With tears in her eyes she thanked me for being open and honest about my own struggles. She thanked me for making her feel "welcome" in the church. Why? Because her past experiences told her that she had to be perfect in order to come. She stopped going to church because she felt like she was too much of a mess. And every person she saw in leadership "had it all together". Only they didn't, and they were too afraid to let anyone know. So, God gave me a chance to be faithful with our youth band at camp so He would know that I could be trusted with the big thing of this woman's heart. And I am honored and humbled that He would even want to use me. I can only pray that I handled her heart well, and that I will do the same for every heart He brings to me in the future.

Pray -

Lord, help me to really understand that the little things are the big things. Help me to really grasp that You care about each individual person, each precious heart, and help me to care about them too. Give me opportunity to be faithful in the small things, and I will trust You to show me how to be faithful in the big things as well. Change my heart so I can reach theirs. In Jesus name, Amen.

Be Still -

Now just sit quietly with God, think about the scripture you read, re-read it if need be. Spend the rest of the 15 minutes just being with God

DAY NINE

Read -
Psalm 3:3

But you, Lord, are a shield around me, my glory, the One who lift my head high.

Thoughts -

For all I have done, for all I have failed to do...I deserve to hang my head. I deserve to hide and be ashamed of myself. But I do not have to. I don't even want to. I want to raise my head as high as I can and raise my voice to the top of my lungs to tell the world what He has done. He is the lifter of my head.

And in those moments when the enemy whispers in my ear and I buy it, even if it's just for a little while, He reminds me whose I am. He takes me by the chin and raises my head up to look Him in the face. He tells me He loves me and has a plan for my life. He is my shield from the fire of the battle. He is the one who points me in the right direction, every single time.

I don't deserve any glory at all, only He is worthy of that. Yet He is my glory.

It is amazing to me that all of the things the world goes after He holds in His hands, and He gives to us so very freely. Yet somehow we think we can attain it all on our own, so we run and strive and ignore His call.

Are you tired of trying to attain it all on your own? Surrender. Right here, right now. Just surrender. Let Him be your glory, let Him lift your head and show you all He has planned for you.

Pray -

Father God, You can have it all. Here it is. I lay down every accomplishment I have run after. I lay down every glory I think I have earned. It is all Yours. I am ready to stop chasing what the world has to offer and to start receiving all You have in store for me. My life, Your plan. My will, Your way. In Jesus mighty name.

Be Still -

Now just sit quietly with God, think about the scripture you read, re-read it if need be. Spend the rest of the 15 minutes just being with God

DAY TEN

Read -
Psalm 37:23-24

The Lord makes firm the steps of the one who delights in Him; though he stumble, he will not fall, for the Lord upholds him with his hand.

Thoughts -

I have been wondering which way to go. I have been looking to the right and to the left...seeking the path He wants my feet on. I can't seem to see a clearly lit way. It frustrates me. I want to know which direction to go. I am actually jealous when I hear someone else say that God has clearly told them what to do in a situation. What??? Come on, God, speak to me!! In the past He has done all but send me a text. He has even had someone else send me a text! But this time...nothing. Just silence. So, I keep looking. I mean, it's okay to keep your eyes open. In fact, I highly recommend it. We need to see our surroundings and be aware of what is happening in our life. But to frantically search is a whole different story. I have been leaning on the frantically searching side. All the while I know for certain He does not want me to be frantic. He wants me to be still. To sit calmly and patiently and wait for Him to lead. He directs the steps of the godly. He actually delights in all of the small details of my life. I don't need to be frantically searching, He has thought of everything. He loves to think of everything that pertains to me. So I can just chill. I can relax and know that He has a plan. All I need to do is seek Him...sit with Him...talk to Him. He is the One who holds it all. He will give me the answers when the time is right.

Are you waiting for an answer in some area of your life? Do you want to see clearly where your foot goes next? Be patient, trust that He is delighting over the plans for your life. Pray, and suddenly the light on the path will shine bright.

Pray -

Lord, I trust You. I will wait patiently for your direction. Lead me in the way You would have me to go. I will stay put until it is made clear. And when You say move, Lord, I will move. In Jesus name, amen.

Be Still -

Now just sit quietly with God, think about the scripture you read, re-read it if need be. Spend the rest of the 15 minutes just being with God.

DAY ELEVEN

Read -
1 Corinthians 9:26-27

Therefore I do not run like someone running aimlessly; I do not fight like a boxer beating the air. No, I stirke a blow to my body and make it my slave so that after I have preached to others, I myself will not be disqualified for the prize.

Thoughts -

I used to be a runner. I LOVED running. Like, seriously loved it. There was this sense of freedom I had every time my Brooks hit the pavement. I would listen to a teaching or worship music and just sense God there with me. I scheduled time for my runs. Especially when I was training for a race. I used an app to map out where I would run that day, it gave me an indication of how long my run would take based on my normal pace. I had a goal of the pace I wanted to have for every run. I never ran aimlessly. Every run was for a purpose. To get better. To feel better. Like Paul said, I never ran like someone running aimlessly.

Do we approach our prayer life this way? Or we do haphazardly mumble out a few sentences in our chaotic morning routine? If we want to live a holy life we have to plan for it. It will not happen by accident. You won't wake up one morning and find that you have overcome all of the things that try to take you down. No way. That's now how it works. But if you carve time out of your day to read the Word, listen to God, ask for direction, things will begin to change. Paul said he makes his body his slave so that he will not disqualify himself in the race. Seems like a weird thing to say, doesn't it? But our spirit is not a slave to our body. Or at least it shouldn't be. Our desires shouldn't be running this show. That's what addiction looks like. No, our body should be a slave to our spirit. So when we think we want something that is not good we can tell our body "no way" and our body will listen.

Pray -

Jesus, your physical body was not in charge of Your life. That is evident in the fact that you surrendered it on the cross for my sins. You came to this earth with purpose and you humbly fulfilled it. Will you please show me how to do the same? Will you show me how to allow my spirit to be led by The Spirit so I can overcome? I pray this in Your name, Lord. Amen.

Be Still -

Now just sit quietly with God, think about the scripture you read, re-read it if need be. Spend the rest of the 15 minutes just being with God.

DAY TWELVE

Read -
Ephesians 6:12

For our struggle is not against flesh and blood, but against the rulers, against the authorities, against the powers of this dark world and against the spiritual forces of evil in the heavenly realms.

Thoughts -

Our struggle. My struggle. Your struggle. We all struggle with something, don't we? My struggle may be shame, while yours may be pride. My struggle may be a substance, yours may be shopping. Our struggles may be different...but they are really all the same. How so? Because our struggles are not against flesh and blood. Nope. They are not. They are against a very real enemy that we cannot even see. Sometimes he is there, present in another person. Sometimes he is whispering in our brain the lies we've been told for so long.

Maybe someone has said something that really hurt you. Firing back at them will not help you at all. You may feel better for a moment, but ultimately it will not help you win your war. Looking at why it hurt, why it affected you and then taking aim at the enemy of your soul with the truth of God's Word will help you win your war. The Bible says the weapons of our warfare are not carnal. They are not anything we can touch with our hands. The Bible says that the Word of God is the sword of the spirit. Our weapon is His Word. In order to fight the enemy we must learn how to wield the sword.

So how do we? How do we wield the sword? We read it, study it, speak it out of our mouth, and pray it. It becomes our first response when we are in a battle. It becomes the one thing we say when trouble comes our way. The more scripture we have memorized, the more weapons we have in our arsenal. So read your Bible people. Memorize scripture. Begin to pray what the Bible says.

Pray -

Today, I am using a scripture as a prayer to show you how to do this...how to literally lift the words off of the page and pray them. This prayer is taken from Ephesians 1 and can be prayed for yourself or someone else.

Lord, would you give me the spirit of wisdom and revelation so that I can know You better. Enlighten the eyes of my heart so I can really know the hope You have called me to, so I can know the incredible riches of this inheritance You have for me, and the incomparably great power You have given me through Your son. As I sit here in Your presence today, Lord, help me to know You better.

Be Still -

Now just sit quietly with God, think about the scripture you read, re-read it if need be. Spend the rest of the 15 minutes just being with God.

DAY THIRTEEN

Read -
Proverbs 22:6

Start children off in the way they should go, and even when they are old they will not turn from it.

Thoughts -

I appreciate the NKJV for this particular scripture. In most other version it says "even when he is old", but the NKJV says "and when he is old". The wording "even when" says that they will still hold to something. But the wording "when he is old" says, maybe not right now...but when they are old. Then.

I have prayed for my children since before they were born. The seeds of the Word of God have been planted in them since the beginning. I may not have always gotten it right as a parent, but I have been very intentional about making sure they know Christ. But something I have realized is that no matter what I say, my children will learn more from what I do. This scripture actually talks about this. Go back and read it again, only this time start at verse 3. It talks about a path -
3 - a prudent or wise man foresees evil and hides from

it. But those who are not wise keep walking on that path.

5 - thorns and snares are on the path of the wicked, but those who guard their soul are far from those things.

6 - train up a child...

Tell them, but walk it too. See the path? Walk in it. Let your child see you walking in it. They will learn from that.

And, honestly, anyone who observes you will learn from it. This week I got two notes thanking me for the way I live. That's not a normal thing...it's not like I get notes all the time telling me how awesome I am. But this week, I needed it. God knew I needed it, so He sent it. But as I read those notes I realized that people are watching. They are either waiting for me to mess up-....or they are waiting to see if this Christianity thing is real so they too can follow.

And isn't that the goal?

Pray -

Lord, help me to lead by example...whether I'm leading my own children or the people I work with. Show me how to light the path that leads to you, so they too can walk it. I fully understand that the goal is for everyone to not depart from the faith, but to live through their old age fully believing, so we can all be with You in eternity. Amen.

Be Still -

Now just sit quietly with God, think about the scripture you read, re-read it if need be. Spend the rest of the 15 minutes just being with God.

DAY FOURTEEN

Read -

Romans 8:28

And we know that in all things God works for the good of those who love him, who have been called according to his purose.

Thoughts -

What is the thing today? What are you facing that you just can't imagine it working out? Guess what...it will. It may not work out the way you envision it, or the way you want it to. It may not end up being anything you had imagined at all. But this scripture says that ALL THINGS work together for GOOD. There is a qualifier on that statement though. All things work together for good for those who love the Lord and are called according to His purpose. So, do you love Him? If so, you are called to fulfill His purpose. And He will work everything in your life out to ensure that His purpose for you is fulfilled...if you let Him. You have to trust Him. You have to know that what this verse says about Him is true. He will work it out for good. Why? Because He is good. He couldn't possibly work it out any other way.

He is good. So what is the thing today? What are you afraid just won't work out. Take it to Him in prayer and then choose to trust Him with it.

Pray -

God, _____ is weighing heavy on my heart today. I just can't seem to see a way through this. But I know You can. I know You have a plan for me, and I know that plan is good. So I will trust You to work this situation out for my good. I love You, Lord. Thank you for calling me and giving me a purpose. I trust You today, in Jesus' name.

Be Still -

Now just sit quietly with God, think about the scripture you read, re-read it if need be. Spend the rest of the 15 minutes just being with God.

DAY FIFTEEN

Read -
Revelation 20:10

And the devil, who deceived them, was thrown into the lake of burning sulfur, where the beast and the false prophet had been thrown. They will be tormented day and night forever and ever.

Thoughts -

Wow, right? Why are we reading this scripture today? Seems a little dark. But it's not. It's really hope. How so? The devil likes to mess with my mind, how about you? He knows my weaknesses, what I struggle with. He likes to suggest to me that whatever situation I am in is going to be the end of me. And when he does, I like to suggest to him that I actually know for certain how this story ends...with him being thrown into the lake of fire and with me in eternity with my Father. And if I'm still here...not there...my story is not over yet. So, when the enemy tries to remind me of my past or my weaknesses, I remind him of his future. And then I remind myself of the fact that the Bible says God has a plan for me and it is good. It includes a future and a hope.

Pray -

Jesus, you died so I could live. You defeated the enemy so I don't have to. Today, I accept that I don't have to. I accept that Your plans for me are good and I don't have to worry about my future. I know how this story ends. Thank you for purchasing my salvation so I can be with You in eternity. My hope is in You.

Be Still -

Now just sit quietly with God, think about the scripture you read, re-read it if need be. Spend the rest of the 15 minutes just being with God.

DAY SIXTEEN

Read -
Romans 8:38-39

For I am convinced that neither death nor life, neither angels nor demons, neither the present nor the future, nor any powers, neither height nor depth, nor anything else in all creation, will be able to separate us from the love of God that is in Christ Jesus our Lord.

Thoughts -

Sometimes I feel as though God's love is nowhere to be found. But according to this scripture it cannot be anything other than close. This says that nothing can separate me from His love. Nothing. Not life or death, or any situation on earth. And certainly not my feelings. As a human being it is so difficult to live like I always have his love because I am so accustomed to being moved by what I feel. It really takes a total mental rehaul to be able to live like I am loved all the time. I'm not there yet. I am working on it, though. The Bible says faith comes by hearing. So I listen. I read the word, and speak it out loud. I listen to teachings every single day...not just on Sundays. I listen to worship music in my car. It's not that I don't think I should listen to other music. I like music of all kinds. But I know that I need to fill my head with the Word so it can fill my heart. Music is just one way I do that. I honestly want all that God has for me. No one else is going to pour that into me. So I have to do it myself. You have to do it yourself. Why? Because when you really understand that His love is always there, always for you, always accessible...it changes the way you live. It causes you to love too. It causes you to give and be all that God has created you to be. So, change the way you think so you can change the way you live.

Pray -

Lord, I want to live like I really know You. I want to live like I really believe everything You say. I am committing today to fill my mind with Your words so I can fill my heart with Your love. I want to love like You do, give like You do, be who You made me to be. I will live like Your love is right here, everyday. In Jesus name.

Be Still -

Now just sit quietly with God, think about the scripture you read, re-read it if need be. Spend the rest of the 15 minutes just being with God.

DAY SEVENTEEN

Read -
2 Corinthians 2:11

in order that Satan might not outwit us. For we are not unaware of his schemes.

Thoughts -

Life is lived differently when we are fully aware of who our enemy is and what he uses against us. Every good war strategist knows that in order to win the war you have to know your enemy. Not that we should give him attention. But we should definitely know his devices. Right before this verse, Paul is talking about forgiveness. Who do we have to forgive? Anyone who offends us. Why? Because offense not forgiven turns into bitterness and resentment...and those are soul wreckers. The enemy never has to lay a hand on you if he can get you to carry unforgiveness in your heart. It will destroy you from the inside out.

But what if you see him for what he is? A liar and a thief. What if you recognize that his devices are unforgiveness, resentment and offense? What if you choose to never take those things on as your own? What if? We could live free. We could overcome and live in peace. It's amazing what forgiveness does for a heart.

As we go into today, do not be unaware of your enemy's devices. He is scheming to destroy you. Recognize him and move on, laying down the things that would trip you up.

Pray -

Lord, I can see where the enemy has tried to get me off track. I can see where he has used my own feelings against me. But I refuse to let him have my joy. Today I choose to forgive, to let go of resentment and regret. I choose to love and extend grace in every area of my life. I am not unaware of the schemes of my enemy, but I am also very aware of the greatness of my God. Where I feel weak, Lord, will you give me strength to overcome. In Jesus name. Amen.

Be Still -

Now just sit quietly with God, think about the scripture you read, re-read it if need be. Spend the rest of the 15 minutes just being with God.

DAY EIGHTEEN

Read -
Romans 4:18-24

Against all hope, Abraham in hope believed and so became the father of many nations, just as it had been said to him, "So shall your offspring be." Without weakening in his faith, he faced the fact that his body was as good as dead - since he was about a hundred years old - and that Sarah's womb was also dead. Yet he did not waiver through unbelief regarding the promise of God, but was strengthened in his faith and gave glory to God, being fully persuaded that God had power to do what he had promised. This is why "it was credited to him as righteousness." The words "it was credited to him" were written not for him alone, but also for us, to whom God will credit righteousness - for us who believe in him who raised Jesus our Lord from the dead.

Thoughts -

It seems impossible, doesn't it? That thing that God is asking of you. It seems like there's no way. Maybe you're not even sure it's Him asking. Because surely He wouldn't be asking YOU to do that. You are not qualified, not good enough, not strong enough, not smart enough, too old, too young, too far gone. Maybe. Maybe you actually are.

But so was Abraham. And he looked that thing right in the face and chose to believe God anyway. That fires me up! Look at verse 19:

Without weakening in his faith, he faced the fact that his body was as good as dead—since he was about a hundred years old—and that Sarah's womb was also dead.

He was like, "Yup, I'm way too old for this...Sarah is waaaaayyyy too old for this." But his faith was not in his own body or Sarah's body. His faith was in the living, breathing God. And NOTHING is too difficult for Him. Verse 21 says Abraham was fully persuaded that God had the power to do what He said.

How persuaded are you? Do you really believe that Jesus is who He says He is? Do you really believe that you are who He says you are? Stop looking in the mirror and allowing the person you see to tell you who God is and is not. Stop letting that person stop you from stepping into God's plan for your life.

Pray -

Jesus, thank you for loving me. Thank you for choosing me and creating me with purpose. Lord, would you help me get beyond my doubt and fear? To see You as You are and me as You made me to be. Would you help me step into all you have planned for me so I can begin to reach a lost and dying world?

Be Still -

Now just sit quietly with God, think about the scripture you read, re-read it if need be. Spend the rest of the 15 minutes just being with God.

DAY NINETEEN

Read -
Proverbs 31:25

She is clothed in strength and dignity; she can laugh at the days to come.

Thoughts -

Oh how I love this one! So much so that I'm going to write it again!

Strength and honor are her clothing, and she can laugh at the time to come!!!

What??? So good!! Strength and honor?? I am clothed with strength and honor! That means that when people look at me THAT is what they see! My friend...YOU are clothed with strength and honor. Why? Because you are a virtuous woman! No? Not you? You've done too much? Then what was Jesus' death for? Oh, you think it was just so you could get into heaven? No. I mean, yes, it does get us into heaven. But that is not all. Unbelievably, amazingly, overwhelmingly, that is not all. He came to give us an abundant life. A life full of joy, peace, and goodness...right here...right now. He died to make you the righteousness of God, in Christ Jesus. So stop dragging your ugly past around with you. Decide today that you are only going to look at the future He has planned for you. He makes you strong, He gives you honor. Not because of who you are or what you do...but because of who HE is and what HE has done for you. Decide that you are going to read the Word, believe the Word, apply the Word to your life today.

So, do it girl. Put on strength and honor today. Wear them with God-confidence. If you need to put on your boots so you can feel it - - do it! Wear the strength and honor He died for you to have. And then laugh. This is my favorite part! Laugh at the future ahead of you. Laugh knowing His plans for you are good and that you and your boots are walking straight into them. No dread here. No dread of what will happen tomorrow. Because even if trouble comes there is still good out ahead of that. His Word says so! Walk in the power and authority of His Word!

Pray -

Jesus, thank you for providing for me a life I could never have dreamed. Thank you for making me whole and pure. Thank you for loving me like that. I don't deserve it, yet You do. As I study your Word would you show me how to live it? Would You help me be more like the person You made me to be? I want to live the power and authority You gave me. In Your mighty name, amen.

Be Still -

Now just sit quietly with God, think about the scripture you read, re-read it if need be. Spend the rest of the 15 minutes just being with God.

DAY TWENTY

Read -
Judges 2:10

After the whole generation had been gathered to their ancestors, another generation grew up who knew neither the Lord nor what he had done for Israel.

Thoughts -

This scripture burns in my heart. I feel responsible to ensure that the next generation knows who God is, who Jesus is. I cannot allow them to die without Him. I have three children of my own. If you have read my book you know what I have walked through with my oldest child. I feel robbed. I feel like the enemy has purposely attacked my family, my child. This is war. No, seriously, this is literally war. It's the spiritual war that we all face every single day. We usually don't even know it's happening. With my child I have very tangible evidence of it. But I also have very tangible evidence of God's saving grace. I see it in my two younger children. I see them seeking...following...even chasing. I see them when they don't know I do - - sitting alone reading their Bibles. I see them playing video games with worship music in their ears. My heart knows the battle is worth the effort.

I also know full well that this war goes beyond the doors of my own home. I continue to see young people who feel overcome by the struggle of this world...the weight too much to bear. I reach out a hand, extend my heart, and swing the sword of the Spirit on their behalf. Some grab on for dear life and let me pull them in. Others turn away and lay down in the muck and the mire of the world around them. There's a Lauren Daigle song called Come Alive that I feel deep in my heart every time I hear it, the lyrics are:

Through the eyes of men it seems there's so much we have lost
As we look down the road where all the prodigals have walked
And one by one the enemy has whispered lies
And led them off as slaves

Ugh...it's like a gut punch. Its painful and frustrating. Because I know that freedom is just beyond the road they walk on. Complete and total freedom. The road they walk on is dark and difficult. But there is a road well lit that would take them to a whole new life. The songs goes on...

But we know that You are God Yours is the victory
We know there is more to come that we may not yet see
So with the faith You've given us
We'll step into the valley unafraid

And so I position myself near the road with eyes and ears open...just waiting for them to see me. Waiting for them to want my hand. This is what we are called to do. To grow in our faith to the point of overcoming our fear so we can extend a hand. You are called to extend a hand. You are called to share the Love of God in an unlovely world...unafraid, unashamed. So the generation yet to come will know that He is God.

Pray -

Lord, help me to live with my eyes wide open, with my ears tuned to hear their cry. Lord, help me understand that my purpose in this life is to lead them to You. Make clear the opportunities you have planned out for me to do so. I commit this morning that I will go. I will do what You have asked of me. In Jesus name.

Be Still -

Now just sit quietly with God, think about the scripture you read, re-read it if need be. Spend the rest of the 15 minutes just being with God.

DAY TWENTY ONE

Read -
Matthew 10:26

So do not be afraid of them, for there is nothing concealed that will not be disclosed, or hidden that will not be made known.

Thoughts -

Have you ever been in a situation where you weren't entirely sure what was happening? Maybe you felt uneasy around a person, but couldn't pinpoint it. I had a situation like this at work a few years back. There was a person who acted one way when with me and a completely different way when there were others around. I knew there was something not right, and it bothered me. But other people just didn't see it. And that bothered me even more. I began to pray about the situation and this scripture came to mind. I started to pray that God would bring what was hidden out into the light.

It didn't happen immediately, and I wanted to talk to others about it. I wanted to point out what I was seeing, but God kept urging me to keep my mouth shut. That can be really hard for an Italian. I actually bought temporary tattoos and put it on my wrist so I could look at it daily. It said, "Be still". Taken from Exodus 14:14 that says:

The Lord will fight for you, you need only be still.

So I waited, put my tattoo on, waited some more, and prayed. "Bring it into the light, Lord." And one day He did. It was no longer just evident to me. And I never had to say a word. And once it became evident, they just chose to move on. I never had to do anything, other than pray, of course. And that really is the best and first defense.

Pray -

Lord, right now I am really struggling with _____. I'm unsure of what to do about it. I can't see the whole story, the whole picture. Would you bring it out of the dark and into the light so I can see clearly what to do? And as I wait, Lord, I will not be afraid. In Jesus name, amen.

Be Still -

Now just sit quietly with God, think about the scripture you read, re-read it if need be. Spend the rest of the 15 minutes just being with God.

DAY TWENTY TWO

Read -
Jeremiah 46:3

Prepare shield and buckler and advance into battle.

Thoughts -

I love this scripture (I say that alot don't I?)! When I first read it I had no idea what a buckler was. So I Googled it! There were YouTube videos of fighters and really in-depth explanations. It was fascinating. Basically both of these things are shields. One is small and one is large. A shield is what you probably imagine it to be. It's a large piece of armor that you wear on your arm to protect yourself. For the most part a shield protects from long-range attack - arrows that are coming from afar. A buckler is a smaller shield that fits right on the hand and it protects from close range attack, as in hand-to-hand combat.

The thing is that you cannot hold both a shield and a buckler at the same time while advancing into battle because you can't hold a weapon if both hands are full. At first I was perplexed by this. But then I read Psalm 91. It says that His faithfulness is our shield AND our buckler. It protects us from far range and close range attacks from our enemy.

This doesn't mean we don't feel the effects of the battle. We do. There's dust and fear and jostling and even falling down. But not death. We don't lose. He holds the shield and the buckler. So we don't have to hold them both. We can simply advance. What does advance mean? To move forward in a purposeful way.

So with His faithfulness protecting us, we can move forward into what He is calling us to - with purpose.

Pray -

Lord, thank you for your strong arm and your hand that protects me. Thank you that You guard me as I move purposefully into Your plan for me. Give me the courage to do all you have called me to. In Jesus name. Amen.

Be Still -

Now just sit quietly with God, think about the scripture you read, re-read it if need be. Spend the rest of the 15 minutes just being with God.

DAY TWENTY THREE

Read

Psalm 91:4

He will cover you with his feathers, and under his wings you will find refuge; his faithfulness will be your shield and rampart.

Thoughts -

I talk alot about being prepared for battle, fighting the good fight of faith, overcoming your enemy. Some days you just can't. I totally get it...some days I just can't. So what do we do then? On the days when we just can't? Where do we go?

We run to Him. He is our refuge, he is our safe place. His faithfulness is our shield and buckler, right? We just read that yesterday. When our heart is hurting and we are just plain worn out from the fight it's okay to re-treat. He covers us with his wings and lets us rest until we have the strength to get up and stand again. Sometimes it takes a little longer than others. But He always knows what we need. He is good, really, really good.

There's a story in 1 Kings 19 about Elijah. He had a really amazing victory where God came through is a huge way. Then his life was threatened and he was afraid. He had all he could stand. The scriptures say he "became afraid." So he ran away and sat down under a tree where he proceeded to ask God to let him die. What happened next is just great. An angel showed up and brought him food and water. He slept and ate...and then slept some more.

So if you are in need of some refuge today run to Him. Eat, sleep, let Him love on you. Curl up in the arms of your Father today.

Pray -

Lord, I feel a little battered and bruised today. I feel like the attacks have come back to back and I cant quite seem to catch my breath. I think I need a time out. I'm running to you, Jesus, would you cover me?

Be Still -

Now just sit quietly with God, think about the scripture you read, re-read it if need be. Spend the rest of the 15 minutes just being with God.

DAY TWENTY FOUR

Read -
Matthew 22:37-39

Jesus replied, "'Love the Lord your God with all your heart and with all your soul and with all your mind.' This is the first and greatest commandment. And the second is like it: 'Love your neighbor as yourself.' All the law and the Prophets hang on these two commandments."

Thoughts -

Christianity can be boiled down to this one scripture...these three little verses...these two points. Love God. Love others. It really is that simple. If we love God, really love Him, it changes everything we do.

If we really love him we will want to know Him better. We will read His Word to learn who He is and what He wants from us. If we really love Him we will love who He loves and we will be better people for it.

The Bible has much to say about love. It covers a multitude of sins, it is kind, it is sacrificial, it is more important than faith. Literally...greater than faith or hope. It is THE primary thing. We simply must love God. We simply must love people. If we do these two things the world will look very different...maybe not to everyone else, but most surely to us.

Pray -

Lord, You love in ways I can't comprehend. You loved me when I was at my worst, I will love you back the best way I can. Teach me to love and give and be more like You. In Jesus' name.

Be Still -

Now just sit quietly with God, think about the scripture you read, re-read it if need be. Spend the rest of the 15 minutes just being with God.

DAY TWENTY FIVE

Read -
Matthew 28:19

Therefore, go and make disciples of all nations, baptizing them in the name of the Father and of the Son and of the Holy Spirit.

Thoughts -

Yesterday's scripture summed up Christianity and today's sums up our purpose as Christians. It's the same for all of us. I mean we each have special gifts and talents that God gave us and wants us to use as we fulfill his plan for our life. But our purpose is all the same. Go and make disciples.

Unfortunately we often tend to leave that to the pastors and church workers. But the truth is that it's our job. We are to go into all the world...our business, our school, the grocery store, our neighborhood...and lead people to Christ. That might scare the heck out of you, but it's really quite simple. It doesn't require anything more than living a life that honors Christ as you do life with them. As they watch you live this Christianity thing out they will begin to notice and you will have opportunity to tell them. Not everyone, but some. And that's all He asks. You can do this, I can do this, we can all do this. We must all do this.

Pray -

Lord, will You help me live a life worthy of You? Will you help me be Christ-like where I live? I want to be an example of Your love, Your grace. So I can win some to You. In Jesus name, amen.

Be Still -

Now just sit quietly with God, think about the scripture you read, re-read it if need be. Spend the rest of the 15 minutes just being with God.

DAY TWENTY SIX

Read -
John 6:1-13

Some time after this, Jesus crossed to the far shore of the Sea of Galilee and a great crowd of people followed him because they saw the signs he had performed by healing the sick. Then Jesus went up on a mountainside and sat down with his disciples. The Jewish Passover Festival was near. When Jesus looked up and saw a great crowd coming toward him, he said to Philip, "Where shall we buy bread for these people to eat?" He asked this only to test him, for he already had in mind what he was going to do. Philip answered him, "It would take more than half a year's wages to buy enough bread for each one to have a bite!" Another one of his disciples, Andrew, Simon Peter's brother, spoke up, "Here is a boy with five small barley loaves and two small fish, but how far will they go among so many?" Jesus said, Have the people sit down." There was plenty of grass in that place and they sat down (about five thousand men were there). Jesus then took the loaves, gave thanks, and distributed to those who were seated as much as they wanted. He did the same with the fish. When they had all had enough to eat he said to his disciples, "Gather the fragments that are left over. Let nothing be wasted."

Thoughts -

I never thought a story about a little boys lunch would speak to my soul the way this one does. I have heard this story seemingly a million times. Jesus fed thousands of people with what should have only fed one little boy. It's amazing, it's incredible. But that's not what sets my heart on fire. No, for me it's the words Jesus spoke at the very end of this story. He said, "gather the fragments (or pieces). Let nothing be wasted." Boom. If you don't feel this deep inside of you, your life must still be intact. But for those of us who have used more duct tape than we'd like to admit, this lights us up.

It lights me up for sure. My heart has been fragmented from past hurts and pain. My life has been taped back together more times than I'd like to admit. But I can get up again when I know that it is not for nothing. I mean, not that He planned for me to fall apart. But He is surely not going to let it be for nothing. He said it Himself, "Let nothing be wasted." Not a single tear, not a single loss. But how? How can such deep pain serve a purpose? This is where it gets good...

When we take our pain and our experiences back to Him, when we hand them over like an offering, He makes something out of them. All of the broken pieces, all of the ashes...He makes something beautiful of it. He uses it to reach into the lives of other people and help them overcome too. For me, it makes it all worth it. It's the thing that makes me say, "No, I wouldn't go back and do it differently." Why? Because I can see the faces of the women whose lives would not be changed if I did. I can see the pain they feel that no one can relate to. My fragments become the tape that Jesus uses to put their hearts back together. So gather the fragments and bring them to Him. Let Him use them for beautiful things.

Pray -

Lord, my heart has been broken over _____. I am bringing the pieces to You. My life has been shattered...I'm bringing the fragments to You. Will you heal me? Will you use my brokenness to help someone else heal, too? Bring them to me and I will share, show me who they are and I will extend Your grace and love. In Jesus name. Amen.

Be Still -

Now just sit quietly with God, think about the scripture you read, re-read it if need be. Spend the rest of the 15 minutes just being with God.

DAY TWENTY SEVEN

Read -
Luke 4:18

The Spirit of the Lord is on me, because he has anointed me to proclaim good news to the poor. He has sent me to proclaim freedom for the prisoners and recovery of sight for the blind, to set the oppressed free, to proclaim the year of the Lord's favor.

Thoughts -

I had to read this scripture, and the one that is now my personal mission statement from Isaiah 61, over and over again before I realized that God was speaking to ME. Yeah, yeah, I know...the prophet was not speaking to Libbie. I get it. I do get it. But God chose to put those words in the book He would give to me years later, for a reason. What would that reason be? For a history lesson? For reference? Maybe. But I am someone who believes those words are there to inspire and speak to me at the times in my life when I most need it. I have read the Bible countless times. Yet, in a moment I will see something that I never saw before, never understood before. It's as though my eyes are opened for the first time to what is written on the page.

In December 2017 I was reading Isaiah 61 and it was as though Jesus was speaking right to me. It was as though He was saying, "My Spirit is on you, Libbie, I have anointed you to go and preach to those who are spiritually poor or dead." So, I read it again, and again, until I understood that, yes, He was sending me. Yes, He has called me. Yes, He has anointed me. He has also anointed, called and is sending you, my friend. Believe it. Jesus Himself said that we would do even greater works than what He did on this earth. That is beyond my ability to grasp, but it helps me to believe that He could be calling me to do anything He chooses...and I don't have to understand it.

So I pick up my Bible and open it, asking Him to speak. I take pen to paper and ask Him what He wants me to share. Your vessel may not be writing or speaking. Yours may be baking or doing taxes. Whatever He has assigned you to, do it with Him leading you. Be Jesus to the world around you right where you are.

Pray -

Lord, I want to be used by You. I really do. I want to share Your love and Your grace every day with the people around me. Show me how to do that. Remind me to read Your Word daily, to talk to You daily. Change me, change my life so I can be more like You and live life more like You.

Be Still -

Now just sit quietly with God, think about the scripture you read, re-read it if need be. Spend the rest of the 15 minutes just being with God.

DAY TWENTY EIGHT

Read -
Mark 11:24

Therefore, I tell you, whatever you ask for in prayer, believe that you have received it, and it will be yours.

Thoughts -

Therefore I tell you whatever you ask in prayer, believe that you have received it and it will be yours.

If you read my book you know at least part of my story. You know that I am a heart broken mom. You know that my oldest child isn't even talking to me right now. As a parent that is one of the most painful things you can face. But I have prayed. I have prayed prayers that have stormed the gates of hell and I believe my answer is on its way.

As a parent of a child with addiction, you deal with something almost like PTSD when it comes to your other children. If you let it, fear can completely take over and make you crazy and irrational. I have found that the only way to face parenting with any sort of normalcy is by leaning completely on God. I mean, that really should be our first choice anyway.

I know I can't control my children's choices or choose their future. I do my best to teach and lead, but ultimately they choose. Tonight I took my two teenagers with me a worship night at a church in Detroit. I get really excited about worship events because I can just pour it all out. As I was doing just that, I looked over and saw my 17 year old daughter on her knees with her hands raised...and my 15 year old son with both hands in the air singing his heart out. Tears filled my eyes and all I could do was thank God for what He has done...for how good He is.

He answers prayers my friend. I have prayed for these children, that they would love Him, that they would choose to worship. They wanted to go to that church tonight...I didn't have to make them. When many teenagers would sit with their arms crossed and not engage, they both poured their hearts out to their Savior. It's the most important prayer that has ever been answered for me. I'm grateful.

Pray -

Lord, I believe you answer prayer. I am praying for _____ tonight. I place it in your hands and I trust you completely, in Jesus name.

Be Still -

Now just sit quietly with God, think about the scripture you read, re-read it if need be. Spend the rest of the 15 minutes just being with God.

DAY TWENTY NINE

Read -
Psalm 27:8

My heart says of you, "Seek his face!" Your face, Lord, I will seek.

Thoughts -

I know this sounds weird, but my heart longs to see God's face. Really. My heart longs to be close to Him. The scene in my living room most mornings is me on the couch, coffee in hand, Bible in lap, dog curled up on the blanket next to me. It feels cozy, looks cute, but my heart is literally burning inside of me to just meet with Him there. What I wouldn't give for a glimpse of His face...a Word from His heart. I know that's where change comes. I know that's where freedom lives. I know adventure is close to Him.

Sometimes I get glimpses. I had coffee with a friend this morning. We met up at Panera, and clutching our cups we excitedly talked about how God worked through her to set another woman free. I saw His face in her. I saw His heart in her. I love to get these glimpses of Him through others. It's just so good.

There's a song called Home by London Gatch. She sings, "Jesus I love to be near you, Jesus I long to spend time with you, Jesus your presence is good for my heart." It is. It's everything my heart needs. I will spend the rest of my life pursuing His face, His presence. If you haven't experienced it let today be your day.

Pray -

Lord, I want more of You. I want to see your face, I want to experience Your presence here with me. Speak through Your Word, move in my life. In Jesus name.

Be Still -

Now just sit quietly with God, think about the scripture you read, re-read it if need be. Spend the rest of the 15 minutes just being with God.

DAY THIRTY

Read -
James 1:5

If any of you lacks wisdom, you should ask God, who gives generously to all without finding fault, and it will be given to you.

Thoughts -

It's not always easy to know how to handle the situations that life throws at us on a day to day basis. Whether we are leading our children, making minor decisions at work or major life choices, the weight of those decisions can bring on a great deal of stress. But the Bible tells us that if we don't have the wisdom for a situation we can ask God for it. It then says He WILL give it to us. He will give us wisdom because He gives to everyone liberally. All we have to do is ask. Then listen.

Oh, right, there's that. If we ask for wisdom we then have to listen for it. So often we close our ears and avert our eyes because wisdom and answers don't always lead us to the easy path. And easy might be more popular than wise. But the end of the wise path is always better than the end of the easier one.

Pray -

Lord, help me to choose wisdom over ease. Help me to listen to You and to do what You say to do. I trust You and I will listen. In Jesus name, amen.

Be Still -

Now just sit quietly with God, think about the scripture you read, re-read it if need be. Spend the rest of the 15 minutes just being with God.

DAY THIRTY ONE

Read -
Matthew 5:6

Blessed are those who hunger and thirst for righteousness, for they will be filled.

Thoughts -

What is righteousness? The quality of being morally correct and justifiable. Can any of us say we are righteous? No. But when we desire to be close to God, we desire to be righteous in His eyes. I have found that the longer I follow Christ the more I want to be like Him. The more time I spend with Him the more I want to please Him. It's funny to me that the biggest heroes of the faith are people who failed morally, who did things that would seemingly keep them far from God. Yet, they were close to Him.

David was called a man after God's own heart. Yet he had an affair and had a guy killed. Abraham was called the father of faith and he lied, slept with another woman, and pretty much gave his wife to some guy. Moses? He got to see God's glory and he literally murdered a guy with his own two hands! But see it's not our behavior that determines if we are blessed. What does this scripture say? Blessed is the person who hungers and thirsts for righteousness. Each of these men desired God. Each of these men chose to surrender, to be obedient even after they had failed, to get closer to God. They were thirsty for the things of God. He satisfied them. They were blessed in many ways.

I would have to say that I am far more morally correct than I was when I first met Jesus. But I still have so far to go. As we follow Him He leads us into a life that looks more like Him. We begin to see our sins for what they are and seek to change how we live. Do you want to be blessed? Develop a desire for more of God. Chase after Him. Desire righteousness and you will be blessed.

Pray -

Lord, my heart longs to be more like You. Will You give me a thirst for Your righteousness? A hunger for the things You want for me? I commit to spend more time with You so that You can work on my heart. In Jesus name, amen.

Be Still -

Now just sit quietly with God, think about the scripture you read, re-read it if need be. Spend the rest of the 15 minutes just being with God.

IN CLOSING

Thank you for spending the month with me. My prayer is that this time has brought you closer to Him. I have seen His hand on my life, and I know that He is no respecter of people. He loves us all the same. His hand is on your life too. Choose today to look for it. Choose today to see Him there, He is there. He loves you and has an incredible plan for your life. Lean into it! Until we study together again - in His love, Libbie.

Made in the USA
Lexington, KY
12 November 2019